HOW TO MASTER STRAREGIC MANAGEMENT IN 24 HOURS

Executives Handbook for Mastering Strategy Planning & Execution

Islam Albelbesy

Contents

Introduction

Even if their strategy is informal, unstructured, and intermittent, all businesses have one. Unfortunately, some organizations do not know in which direction they are headed. The proverb "If you don't know where you're going, any road will get you there" emphasizes businesses' need to use strategic-management principles and procedures. Small businesses, major corporations, non-profit organizations, government agencies, and global conglomerates increasingly use the strategic management method. The practice of empowering managers and workers offers almost endless advantages.

In their business, organizations should adopt a proactive rather than a reactive strategy, and attempt to influence, foresee, and initiate rather than just react to events. The practice of strategic management incorporates this approach to decision-making.

It is a rational, systematic, and objective way to define the future path of a business. The stakes are often too significant for strategists to rely on their intuition when deciding between various courses of action. Successful strategists take the time to consider their companies, where they are with their enterprises, and where they want to be as organizations; they then execute programs and policies to go from where they are to where they want to be within a realistic time frame.

People and organizations who plan are far more likely to achieve their goals than those that do not plan. A competent strategist plans and controls their plans, but a poor strategist never plans and then attempts to manage others! This work is dedicated to equipping you with the knowledge and skills required for.

About the Author

Islam is a dynamic Senior Management Consultant with a proven track record in crafting and executing high-impact strategies. His expertise spans Digital Transformation, Shared Service Centre optimization, Project Management Offices, Business Process Engineering, and Governance.

Key Expertise:
Strategy and Vision: Crafting and implementing strategic visions that drive organizational success. Islam's approach involves aligning business objectives with actionable strategies to propel companies forward in today's dynamic landscape.

Digital Transformation: As a digital transformation expert, Islam empowered organizations to embrace innovation, harness digital technologies, and stay ahead of industry trends. while being passionate about creating agile and digitally resilient enterprises.

Shared Service Centre: Proficiency in designing, implementing and optimizing Shared Service Centres with massive focus on creating collaborative ecosystems that enhance service delivery, reduce costs, and elevate overall organizational performance.

Project Management Offices (PMO): Leveraging experience in Project Management, Islam thrive in establishing and leading Project Management Offices. His commitment is to ensure seamless project execution aligned with strategic goals.

Business Model & Organizational Design: Crafting innovative business models and designing effective organizational structures through alignment with strategic goals and creating agile organizational designs that drive performance and optimize resource utilization.

Business Process Engineering: Specializes in streamlining operations through diligent business process engineering. By optimizing workflows and empowering organizations to enhance operational efficiency, reduce redundancies, and adapt to evolving market demands.

Governance: Advocates for robust structures that ensure compliance, risk mitigation, and ethical business practices. Focused on creating governance frameworks that foster transparency, accountability, and sustainable growth.

Commercial Arbitration: Utilizing financial expertise to the field of commercial arbitration, navigating legal landscapes and facilitating fair resolutions. Committed to meticulous analysis and strategic thinking ensures the best outcomes for all parties involved among the arbitration sessions/tribunals.

Academic Tuition: Beyond professional endeavours, Islam's passion is about education. As an experienced academic tutor, He had the privilege of nurturing the growth and development of students among different age ranges and different career levels.

 @IslamAlbelbesy
 @IslamAlbelbesy

CHAPTER 01

The Fundamentals

Understand aspects of Strategy

Section 01

Strategic Management - Know the Purpose, Importance, Definition, & Process

Strategic Management - Know the Purpose, Importance, Definition, & Process

Strategy derives from the Greek word "stratigos," which means "general," i.e., a military leader or commander. Modernly, this word refers to an overall strategy for reaching one or more unknown long-term objectives. Every organization has its own set of aims and goals. These goals and objectives are established by the organization's capacity and desire for growth. However, achieving these objectives is insufficient, and the absence of strategic vision incurs exorbitant expenses. Therefore, the organization must take the appropriate actions to achieve these objectives. These measures are referred to as the company's strategy.

• Definition of Strategic Management

Strategic Management is described as the creation and execution of the organization's key objectives and efforts on behalf of its associates, considering the organization's internal and external work cultures. It often consists of the organization's objectives, goals, and policies that reflect its extreme level.

• What Is Strategic Management?

Strategic management is the art of creating, executing, and assessing multifunctional strategies that enable businesses to attain their goals. It is a continuous process of formulating and executing strategies to attain objectives. This helps in splitting significant objectives into smaller, more manageable objectives. With effective plan development and execution, reaching the objectives becomes simple. The primary goals of strategic management are twofold.

1. To obtain a competitive edge, outperform the competition, and attain market domination, and
2. To serve as a guide for the firm is adapting to the changing business environment.

Strategic management includes establishing organizational goals, monitoring rivals' activities, reassessing the organization's internal structure, analysing current strategies, and confirming the company-wide execution of these strategies. Strategic planning is a mix of strategic thinking. Strategic planning is the identification of attainable objectives. Strategic thinking is identifying the needs necessary for an organization to achieve the objectives identified via strategic planning.

Two forms of strategic planning exist: prescriptive and descriptive. Former strategic management is formulating organizational strategies in advance of a problem. In descriptive strategic management, strategies are developed as required. While most organizations' senior management executes the strategy, some hire strategists who develop and implement the strategy to enhance corporate performance.

• What Is the Purpose of Strategic Management?

Strategic management provides firms a competitive advantage and assists in attaining their objectives. This provides the performance a future appearance, and the expansion becomes sustainable. Additionally, it helps unite workers and management, resulting in a cohesive workplace.

Strategic management is an ongoing process of designing and executing strategies to accomplish objectives. This aids in splitting large plans into smaller, more manageable objectives. With effective plan development and execution, reaching the objectives becomes simple. It helps every company arrange its objectives more clearly. Therefore, it is regarded as both a talent and an art. Strategic management is considered a talent since the approaches may be learned as an area of knowledge. On the other hand, it is also considered an art since it involves evaluating and contemplating an unknown future. Every firm must thus include strategic administration into its management procedures.

• Why is Strategic Management Necessary?

Strategic management assists the person in charge of decision-making in securing management tools or anticipating organizational changes by directing organizational operations in the proper direction. In addition, the strategic management technique reduces operational risk by aiding the firm in innovating and acting in advance. Listed below are the reasons why strategic management is essential to a firm.

1. *Helps To Anticipate the Changes*

As stated before, strategic management necessitates that the manager analyses the company's future and the market. Continuously investigating the future, Managers can foresee the shift. When executed correctly, strategic management may lead a business to respond to or cause a market shift. Strategic management enables businesses to make choices based on detailed projections rather than rash responses. It helps the company take action early on a new trend and estimate the lead time for effective management.

2. *Clarity In Objectives and Direction*

Strategic management provides workers and management with a powerful incentive to achieve organizational goals. In addition, strategic management ensures that the senior executives have a unified view of strategic issues.

3. *Increases Employee Efficiency*

All levels of staff participate in the strategic management process. As a consequence, workers are more motivated and involved in their job. The workers get the necessary training, and the employees carry out the inter-process of strategy implementation. This boosts the productivity of the workforce. A strategic workflow enhances organizational performance management. When workers believe they are essential to achieving the organization's objectives and are a part of the organization's larger vision, they will be willing to provide their best effort.

4. *Rises Profitability*

Profitability of the business unit is contingent upon maximizing the usage of available resources. With strategic management, managers may maximize financial resources and labour capacity to raise the unit's production and profitability.

5. *Reduces Expenses*

Strategic management enables the firm to spend less on unneeded expenditures. For instance, a company's fixed capital is the amount invested in its fixed assets. With strategic management, managers can determine if it would be more advantageous to invest in these fixed assets or rent them to reduce their fixed capital investment.

6. Fills The Organizational Gap

An organizational gap is a departmental task for which no person is responsible. No employee may be held accountable if such an allocation is omitted by accident. Due to the process of strategic management's ongoing engagement and communication, every employee gets equal effort. Due to this, organizational gaps that impede a company's capacity to achieve its objectives may be eliminated. With strategic management, this obstacle may be overcome.

- ## Interesting Facts to Know About Strategic Management

Over 97% of employers believe that strategy execution is more difficult than strategy design.

Sixty-seven percent of employers claim that their firms create the most effective strategies. However, only approximately 45% to 47% of their implementations are successful.

More than 65% of the plans devised fail due to improper execution.

While 18% of companies indicate that finding people with the requisite abilities to drive the execution of the plan is a top priority, 11% are developing and upgrading these skills in their current workforce.

More than sixty percent of organizations with a systematic framework for managing strategic choices have outperformed their rivals.

Twenty percent of businesses examine the implementation of their strategic decisions weekly.

Approximately 4% of the potential of strategic management is squandered owing to the absence of specified responsibilities.

Section 02

How is Strategy Formulated?

How is Strategy Formulated?

Strategic management requires an investment in strategic planning. Strategic planning represents an organization's capacity to identify the steps necessary to achieve its short- and long-term objectives. Here are the seven phases of the strategic management process:

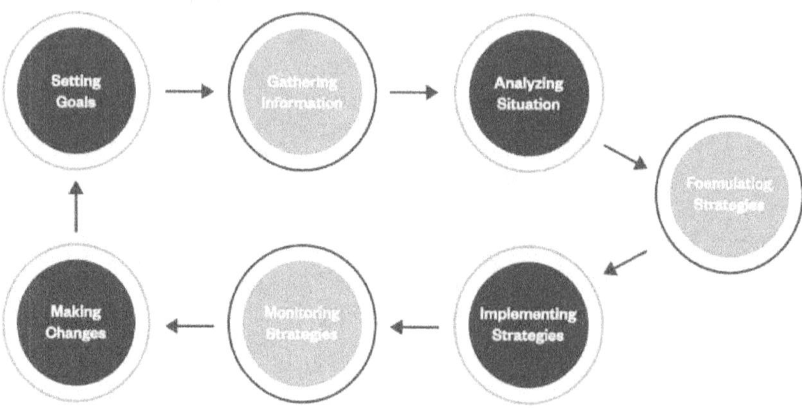

- ## Setting A Goal

The first step of strategic management is establishing the company's objectives. This stage involves establishing both long-term and short-term objectives. The management should then communicate these objectives to the whole company and explain how they will affect its future. Each team member has a feeling of purpose and engagement in their work.

- ## Gathering the Information

The next step is collecting all pertinent data. This information will be essential to the vision and objectives of the organization. Questions requiring replies include potential future changes, the company's market share, the market share of its rivals, etc.

- ## Analysing the Situation

After collecting the essential data and outlining their vision and objective, the next step is to examine the current condition. This phase analyzes the company's internal and external settings and evaluates its rivals. Using all the available information, managers should classify all the data according to its relevance to the present scenario.

- **Formulating The Strategy**

The management must design the plan after comprehensively analyzing the data and the circumstances. The resulting plan should be transparent and straightforward. Lacking a strategy is preferable to having a vague one since a lack of direction among personnel leads to inefficiency and confusion.

- **Implementing The Strategy**

Implementing the approach is the best method for determining its success. At this level, the most important talents are management skills. The strategy must be communicated, along with describing each employee's responsibility. The new design must have organization-wide support to be properly implemented.

- **Monitoring The Strategy**

After implementation, it is vital to monitor the approach's success continuously. But first, the management must determine if the plan is effective. The ideas should be executed regularly after testing them on a smaller scale. This promotes constant development, aids in staff retention, and has a no larger impact on the firm. Additionally, you may effectively supervise your staff at a lesser level.

- **Making Changes**

If the approach has unintended consequences, the management should review it and make the required adjustments. Alternatively, if the process runs well, the manager might predict future issues and devise solutions if the process runs well.

Section 03

Types of Strategic Management that are commonly habituated

Types of Strategic Management that are commonly habituated

Some considerations must be made and kept in mind while formulating a plan to perform better. Such as the organization's primary objective, future objectives, and the best method to distinguish itself from the competition. After these goals have been accomplished, various business tactics may help you remain realistic and expand your market share. Several of these are detailed below:

- **Structuralist Strategy**

Utilizing the industry's structure to your advantage. A structuralist approach is constructing a firm around the current market space while maximizing the industry's structure. For instance, a corporation is executing a plan to boost the present product's sales.

- **Growth Strategy**

When a firm releases new goods or features or enters a new market, a growth plan is executed. For instance, adding an online component to a corporation that already exists in the offline world might be one of an organization's development strategies.

- **Mover Advantage Strategy**

A product or business receives an advantage by providing a certain service or product first. For instance, eBay is the first online auction site that matches all sorts of customers and sellers.

- **Leader Strategy (Red Ocean Strategy)**

A cost leader approach is a method for establishing your product's competitive price, which distinguishes your product from that of competitors. Therefore, you may charge the lowest possible price for a product while being flexible and profitable. Amazon, for instance, employs a cost leadership approach by offering extensive warehouse facilities, reducing physical scale economies.

- ## **Differentiation Strategy (Blue Ocean Strategy)**

Differentiation permits your company to occupy a creative area by providing a unique product, charging for the innovative product, and establishing a premium segment for your goods. Since its inception, Apple has been a product with distinctive product design, operating system, and other distinguishing characteristics.

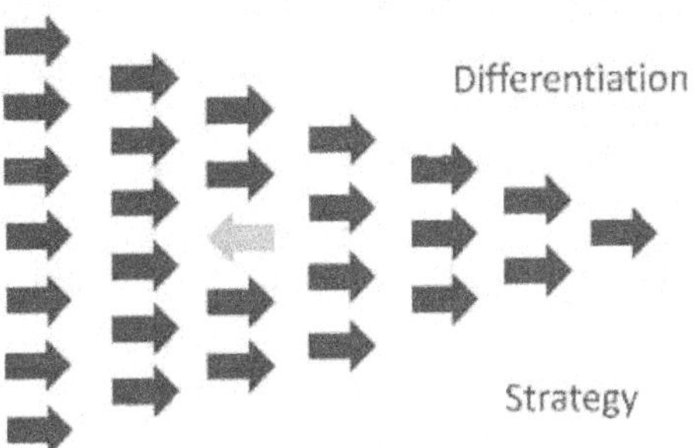

- ## **Price-Skimming Strategy**

The method of price skimming entails pricing a product inside the original range to pay the manufacturing, marketing, and product costs. Subsequently, when comparable items are released, the price range is decreased relative to the original cost to maintain the product's competitive advantage. For example, when Nike's items were first introduced, they were priced more to attract customers who needed them. However, when the price reduces, sales remain steady since the lower price attracts consumers.

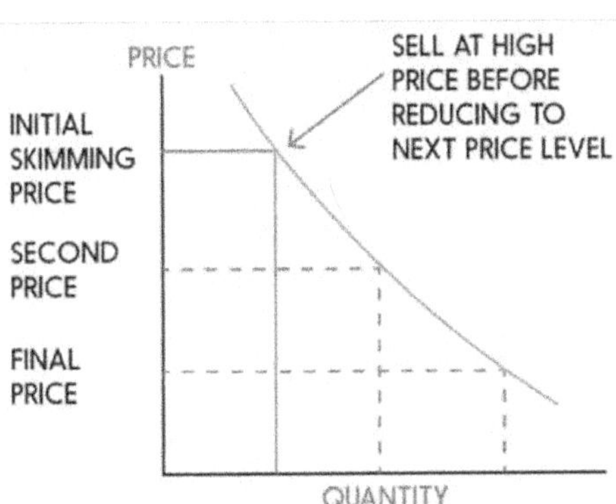

- **Acquisition Strategy**

The acquisition strategy encourages the growth of a product by acquiring and controlling another product. Legal and financial experts might be useful members of your team, even though some situations can be complicated. Sephora's social media efforts and influence marketing are the true illustration of this technique.

- **Focus Strategy**

A focus strategy targets a market sector using the previously mentioned techniques. However, it is occasionally advantageous to concentrate on a certain segment rather than the whole market. For instance, Coca-diet-coke Cola's was one of the most ingenious items that pushed the company to diabetics and others who like low-sugar drinks.

CHAPTER 01

The Fundamentals

Understand aspects of Strategy

Section 04

Key Terms in Strategic Management

Key Terms in Strategic Management

Before discussing strategic management in further detail, we must define nine basic terms: competitive advantage, strategists, vision and mission statements, external opportunities and threats, internal strengths and weaknesses, long-term goals, strategies, yearly objectives, and policies.

• Competitive Advantage

Competitive advantage is the primary objective of strategic management. This concept may be described as "everything that a company does better than its competitors." When a company can accomplish something that its competitors cannot or has something that its competitors won't, it may have a competitive edge. For instance, having adequate cash on the balance sheet might give a significant competitive advantage in a worldwide economic slump. Some cash-rich companies are acquiring struggling competitors. For instance, BHP Billiton, the biggest mining company in the world, is attempting to acquire competing companies in Australia and South America. Freeport-McMoRan Copper & Gold Inc. seeks to grow its portfolio by acquiring troubled competitors. Sanofi-Aventis SA, a French pharmaceutical corporation, is purchasing troubled rivals to increase its medication research and diversification. Johnson & Johnson in the United States, flush with cash, is also purchasing ailing competitors. This may be an effective tactic during a worldwide economic downturn.

• Strategists

The person most responsible for an organization's success or failure is its strategists. Strategists have several job titles, including a chief executive officer, president, owner, board chair, executive director, chancellor, dean, and entrepreneur. Professor of organizational behavior at the London Business School and author of Building Leaders Jay Conger asserts, "All strategists must serve as chief learning officers. We are through a protracted era of transformation. If our leaders are not extremely adaptable and excellent role models during this moment, then neither will our organizations, since leadership is ultimately about being a role model."
Strategists aid organizations in collecting, analyzing, and organizing information. They monitor industry and competitive trends, construct forecasting models and scenario studies, analyze corporate and divisional

performance, discover new market opportunities, recognize business dangers, and devise innovative response strategies. Typically, strategic planners' function in a support or staff capacity. They are often found at upper levels of management and have extensive decision-making influence inside the organization. The chief executive officer is the most visible and crucial strategic manager. A strategic manager is any manager accountable for a unit or division, responsibility for profit and loss results, or direct control over a substantial portion of the firm (strategist). In the last five years, numerous firms, including Sun Microsystems, Network Associates, Clarus, Lante, Marimba, Sapient, and Commerce One, have added the role of chief strategy officer (CSO) to their executive management teams.

- **Vision and Mission Statements**

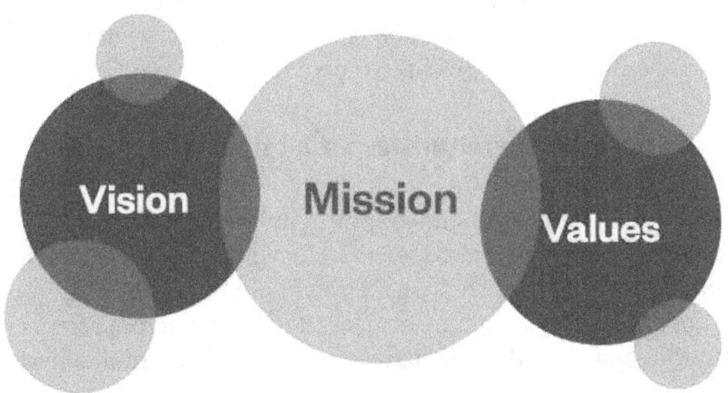

Vision and Mission Statements: Nowadays, businesses create a vision statement addressing the issue, "What do we want to become?" Creating a vision statement is often seen as the first stage in strategic planning, even before formulating a mission statement. Numerous vision statements consist of just a single phrase. The mission statement of the Stokes Eye Clinic in Florence, South Carolina, for instance, is "Our goal is to care for your eyesight."

Mission statements are "enduring declarations of purpose that differentiate one company from other businesses of a like kind." A mission statement defines the product and market scope. It answers the fundamental question all strategists must: "What is our business?" A concise mission statement conveys the organization's beliefs and goals. Creating a mission statement requires strategists to consider the nature and breadth of current operations and the potential allure of future markets and activities. A mission statement outlines the general future course of an organization. A mission statement reminds workers of the organization's raison d'être and what its founders envisioned when they risked their fame and money to bring their ambitions to reality. Here is a fight Barnes & Noble's mission statement is that our goal is to run the best-specialized retail store in the United States, regardless of our products. Because of the commodity, we offer books; our goals must align with the promises and ideals of the volumes on our shelves. To assert that our purpose exists apart from the thing we sell is to diminish the significance and distinctiveness of being bookstores. As bookstores, we are committed to becoming the greatest in our industry, regardless of the size, lineage, or preferences. We will continue applying industry-specific peculiarities of style and methods to bookselling that align with our changing goals. Above all else, we want to be a credit to the communities we serve, a valued resource to our customers, and a place where our devoted booksellers may flourish. To achieve this objective, we will not only listen to our customers and booksellers but also embrace the notion that the company exists to serve them.

• External Opportunities and Threats

Economic, social, cultural, demographic, environmental, political, legal, governmental, technical, and competitive developments and events that might greatly help or hurt an organization in the future are examples of external opportunities and dangers. Thus, the term external refers to opportunities and risks that are mainly outside the control of a particular business.

• Internal Strengths and Weaknesses

Internal strengths and weaknesses are the controllable operations of an organization that are executed exceptionally effectively or badly. They occur in management, marketing, finance/accounting, production/operations, research and development, and management information systems. Identifying and assessing organizational strengths and weaknesses in a company's functional domains is a key strategic management exercise. Organizations aim to adopt strategies that maximize their internal strengths and remove internal flaws. Determine strengths and weaknesses compared to the competition. Relative inferiority or superiority is crucial information. Additionally, strengths and weaknesses may be judged by aspects g as opposed to performance. For instance, a strength may be possessing natural resources or an enduring reputation for excellence. A company's strengths and weaknesses might be judged according to its goals. High inventory turnover levels, for instance, may not be a positive for a company that strives to never run out of product.

External influences may be determined in various methods, including calculating ratios, monitoring performance, and comparing historical eras and industry norms. Internal aspects like staff morale, production efficiency, advertising efficacy, and consumer loyalty may also be examined via the development and administration of various surveys.

- **Long-Term Objectives**

In fulfilling its fundamental goal, an organization's objectives are the particular outcomes it tries to attain. Long-term is defined as beyond one year. Objectives are vital to the success of an organization because they give direction, help in assessment, foster synergy, disclose priorities, concentrate coordination, and serve as a foundation for successful planning, organizing, motivating, and regulating operations. The objectives should be difficult, quantifiable, consistent, reasonable, and transparent. In a multidimensional organization, both general and divisional goals should be created.

- **Annual Objectives**

Annual targets are short-term benchmarks businesses must fulfill to attain long-term goals. Like long-term goals, yearly goals should be quantifiable, demanding, attainable, consistent, and prioritized.

- **Policies**

The mechanisms by which yearly goals are attained are policies. Policies consist of set standards, regulations, and procedures that support attempts to attain specified goals. Policies serve as decision-making aids and handle recurrent or repeating circumstances.

Policies are often described in management, marketing, finance/accounting, production/operations, research/development, and computer information system activities. Policies may be set at the corporate level for a whole company, at the divisional level for a single division, or the functional level for specific operational activities or departments. Policies, like yearly goals, are crucial to successfully executing a strategy since they establish an organization's employee and management Expectations. Policies facilitate cohesion and collaboration between and within organizational divisions.

CHAPTER 01

The Fundamentals

Understand aspects of Strategy

Section 05

Principles of Strategic Management

Principles of Strategic Management

- ## **Competitive Advantage**

A company may attain a reduced manufacturing cost or product distinctiveness. It is essential to consider the brand's and business's market positioning and identify any competitive advantages the firm has over its rivals.

- ## **Corporate Strategy and Portfolio Theory**

Modern Portfolio Theory offers a framework for allocating assets to optimize anticipated return for a given degree of risk. Portfolio Theory enables organizations to do a cost-benefit analysis on the deployment of resources and evaluate the overall value of each resource placement. The Growth-Share Matrix, created by the Boston Consulting Group, assists organizations in analyzing the value of their separate business units by arranging them along an axis. The two criteria for evaluation are market share – a measure of a business unit's competitive position relative to its competitors – and industry growth rate – a measure of the unit's industry prospects.

- ## **Core Competence**

Businesses should acquire expertise in relative superiority while eliminating or outsourcing most of their operations. By being able to do so, an organization may provide the market and customers with a product, service, or viewpoint that is unique and unmatched.

- ## **Experience Curve**

The experience curve demonstrates that anytime production doubles, value-added costs decrease by a constant proportion.

CHAPTER 01

The Fundamentals

Understand aspects of Strategy

Section 06

Framework for Strategic Management

Framework for Strategic Management

- ## Porter's 5 Forces

The Competitive Forces Model (Porter's 5 Forces) is used to evaluate the industry's competitiveness.

- ## Threat of new entrants

In a competitive industry, new entrants pose a significant danger. Assuming an industry or area is very lucrative, many may see it as an exciting business opportunity. Patents, expensive financial requirements, consumer loyalty to established brands, and current economies of scale deter market entrance.

- ## Threat of substitutes

If a comparable alternative can readily replicate a product or event, we say its demand has been diluted. If customers have access to comparable alternatives.

- ## Bargaining power of customers

In a competitive market, the bargaining power of customers will be significant. Sellers will be unable to apply price pressure that is profitable for them.

- ## Bargaining power of suppliers

When several vendors are available to provide raw or intermediate materials, they cannot unfairly affect the ultimate price.

- ## Competitive rivalries

Competitive sectors are characterized by a high level of innovation and advanced marketing and competitive tactics.

- **SWOT Analysis**

The acronym SWOT refers to strengths, weaknesses, opportunities, and threats. This technique permits the investigation of both internal and external influences. Internal factors include positive (strengths) or negative (weaknesses) factors that exist within your organization and can be changed or influenced in some way, whereas external factors include positive (opportunities) or negative (threats) factors that exist outside the subject you are evaluating and cannot be changed or influenced by you or your organization.

Strengths	Weaknesses
Characteristics of a business which give it advantages over its competitors	Characteristics of a business which make it disadvantageous relative to competitors
Opportunities	Threats
Elements in a company's external environment that allow it to formulate and implement strategies to increase profitability	Elements in the external environment that could endanger the integrity and profitability of the business

- **Balanced scorecard**

A balanced scorecard aids in determining which aspects of a healthy need development by dividing the performance review process into four distinct regions, or "legs." These legs consist of:

- Learning and expansion,
- Business operations,
- Viewpoints, and
- Financial data.

The balanced scorecard approach may provide timely reporting systems that display all firm growth-related facts.

- **Value Chain**

The value chain is a list of procedures or actions performed by a corporation to get a product or service to market. The activities consist of two functions:

1. *Primary activities*

These are activities that directly contribute to producing a product or service. They include tasks including incoming and outgoing logistics, operations, marketing and sales, and product service.

2. *Supporting activities*

These functions support manufacturing the product or service. They include human resources, information technology, procurement, and infrastructure.
According to Porter, coordinating activities may increase an organization's operational efficiency and eventually provide it with a competitive edge.

Section 07

Approaches of Effective Business Strategy

Approaches of Effective Business Strategy

- ## Fresh Thinking & Visioning

Always guarantee that the approach is influenced and informed by novel ideas. Too often, strategy is formulated by business experts who fail to adopt a new viewpoint. If you continue to think as you always have, you will continue to get the same results.

Introduce some forward-thinking fresh blood into the organization and give them a "license" to question the status quo. Invite impartial specialists to participate in the process acceptably. In this regard, strategic relationships may also be used.

It will be worthwhile to spend some time seeing the future, even if just a tiny fraction of the overall time spent. Imagining the future advancement of technology and how it may affect your consumers' attitudes and behaviors and how they purchase and use your products/services may broaden your perspective and provide insight into the market dynamics and conventions in which your company will operate.

- ## Data and information provision

Do not underestimate the time necessary to collect the necessary facts and information to provide a strong foundation and insight to support and guide strategic alternatives and direction. It is often neglected, placing undue strain on the schedule and compromising the quality of insights and decisions. It will undoubtedly need more cash. Therefore, it may be bundled with the strategic process investment.

- ## Resourcing strategy preparation effectively

Regarding the time and resources necessary to build the strategy, I found it advantageous to manage the expectations of stakeholders and all those participating in the strategic process. Typically, a timetable with milestones is practical. Ensure that the right individuals are engaged or have input, and strategic planning activities are supported or have access to a budget.

- **Connect with the right people throughout the business**

Great ideas and novel insights may originate from any place in an organization. The ability is in identifying the appropriate individuals and including them in the process at the time when they can provide the most value, and not necessarily during the whole preparation period. I've discovered that it works well to have individuals attend certain seminars at specified times and then allow them to remain engaged by offering ideas remotely after the session.

- **Input to drive ownership**

Take advantage of the opportunity to engage individuals who will advocate the plan throughout the enterprise, bringing it to life and pushing its execution. This fosters ownership and faith. A plan cannot be exceptional unless the whole organization strongly believes in it.

CHAPTER 01

The Fundamentals

Understand aspects of Strategy

Section 08

Components of a Successful Business Strategy

Components of a Successful Business Strategy

A business strategy synthesizes three elements: declared corporate goals, target market identification, and strategic management strategies. These factors align to put the organization in a competitive position to fulfill its short- and long-term business objectives.

- **Business objectives**

If the entire company plan is a road map, then business goals are success checkpoints along the way. Business objectives may be short-term, medium-term, or long-term. Short-term objectives include official incorporation, the employment of a corporate-level staff, creating a vision statement, and selling the first batch of goods or services. Medium-term objectives might include releasing a new technology or items, claiming a particular market share, producing a smartphone application, or topping consumer satisfaction polls. Long-term aims may include an initial public offering (IPO), reaching a specified revenue goal, acquiring a rival, or being bought by a major company.

- **Target market identification**

This aspect of business strategy is identifying the consumers of your product or service. In a well-crafted business plan, a firm will determine if another brand is supplying these prospective consumers, how they might be lured away from that brand, and what they need in exchange for their allegiance. These will guide your future marketing efforts.

- **Strategic management plans**

These are the business strategies your organization will use to attain its commercial goals using the defined target market. This category includes a brand's marketing strategy (how will it interact with new consumers?), competitive strategy (what are all the potential income streams?), and growth plan (how will it claim current markets and then reach target customers in new marketing idea while establishing a strategic course so that all company operations contribute to the achievement of the brand's business goals.

CHAPTER 01

The Fundamentals

Understand aspects of Strategy

Section 09

Benefits of Strategic Management

Benefits of Strategic Management

Planning and perseverance are required to achieve organizational objectives. Strategic management may aid businesses in achieving their objectives. Strategic management guarantees company-wide implementation of the actions required to achieve a business objective. Strategic management provides several advantages to businesses that use it, including

- ### Competitive advantage

Strategic management provides firms with a competitive edge over rivals since its proactive approach ensures that organizations are always informed of market changes.

- ### Achieving goals

Strategic management facilitates the attainability of objectives by using a transparent and dynamic procedure to formulate and execute stages.

- ### Sustainable growth

It has been shown that strategic management results in more efficient organizational performance, which leads to controllable expansion.

- ### Cohesive organization

Strategic management requires company-wide communication and goal execution. It is more probable that an organization will accomplish a goal if its members work in sync with that objective.

- ### Increased managerial awareness

Strategic management requires a focus on the organization's future. If managers routinely do this action, they will be more aware of industry trends and obstacles. They will be better equipped to meet future issues using strategic planning and thinking.

CHAPTER 01

The Fundamentals

Understand aspects of Strategy

Section 10

How does Strategic Management works?

How does Strategic Management works?

Strategic management includes establishing organizational goals, assessing the activities of rivals, examining the organization's internal structure, evaluating existing plans, and ensuring company-wide implementation.

Strategic management can be prescriptive or descriptive.

- **Prescriptive**

Strategic management involves the creation of strategies in advance of an organization's problem.

- **Descriptive**

Strategic management involves implementing strategies as necessary.

Both strategic management approaches utilize management theory and practices. While higher management is accountable for executing plans, any employee may provide ideas, objectives, or organizational issues. Numerous businesses hire strategists whose job is to think and plan strategically to enhance corporate performance.

- **Five steps of Strategic Management**

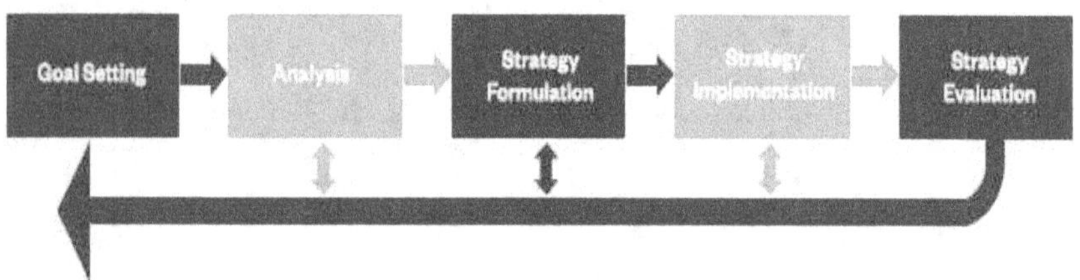

While there are several methodologies and frameworks for strategic management, the process usually consists of five steps:

1. Identification
2. Analysis
3. Formation
4. Execution
5. Evaluation

1. *Identification*

The first phase in strategic management is evaluating the present direction of the organization. Typically, this involves knowing the company's objective, purpose, and overarching strategic direction. Assessing where the organization's present method will assist you in achieving your objective.

2. *Analysis*

Once you have a firm grasp of the existing procedure, you must assess its specifics. What is effective? What is not working? What feedback can you get from organizational stakeholders? Now is the moment to respond to any inquiries that may assist cement the strategic plan's essential components. A SWOT analysis, or assessing a business's strengths, weaknesses, opportunities, and threats, is a valuable tool.

3. *Formation*

Once you have the necessary facts, it is time to construct an action plan for achieving the objective. Ensure that the stages are distinct, focused, and directly tied to the objective. If the process or method will affect many employees inside the company, provide clear implementation instructions.

4. *Execution*

Follow the actions described in your plan of action. Ensure that all stakeholders execute the strategy according to its specifications for optimal efficiency.

5. *Evaluation*

Analyze the finished result. Did you reach your goal? Was the procedure adopted adequately throughout the organization? Based on your responses to these questions, you may ponder and amend them as necessary.

- ## **Example of strategic management**

1. Identification

Wood's Fine Furnishings is ready to launch a brand-new collection of kitchen tables. They decided to employ strategic management to guarantee that the product launch is executed smoothly, effectively, and uniformly across all of their retail locations.

2. Analysis

Wood's Fine Furnishings has had uneven marketing and erroneous shipping prices in the past with the debut of new goods at their many retail locations. Before releasing their new range of kitchen tables, they've chosen to do a SWOT analysis to identify areas for improvement.

Strengths	Weaknesses	Opportunities	Threats
<ul><li>Excellent stuff,</li><li>Multiple locations for the convenience of buying,</li><li>Simple shipping cost</li></ul>	<ul><li>inadequate communication between shop management and staff,</li><li>Multiple shipping rates are imposed at certain shops,</li><li>Unreliable marketing approach</li></ul>	<ul><li>Integrated marketing,</li><li>Transparent fees</li></ul>	<ul><li>The primary rival of Wood's Fine Furnishings debuted a range of kitchen tables last quarter.</li></ul>

3. Formation

Wood's Fine Furnishings designs a strategic strategy for launching their kitchen tables using their SWOT analysis. It entails supplying uniform print and digital marketing materials to all retail locations. In addition, a representative will be dispatched to each retail location to explain how to apply the shipping fee to all orders accurately. Finally, the support team implements an internal message system so that store managers may communicate efficiently and effectively about issues and achievements in their shops.

4. *Execution*

One month before the launch of the new kitchen tables, the marketing team distributes promotional materials to all retail locations. Every shop receives instructions on how to deploy the marketing materials properly. Store managers are taught about the new message system two weeks before the rollout. The trainers handle inquiries and ensure that each manager configures the messaging service on their corporate mobile phone and office PC.
A week before the launch, a company headquarters representative instructs each store staff on how to calculate shipping fees for a transaction correctly. Managers are also there to ensure the proper execution of this procedure with consumers.

5. *Evaluation*

One month following the first day of sales, Wood's Fine Furnishings evaluates the kitchen table release statistics. They discovered that the marketing strategy pushed buyers to the nearest retail store to see the tables in person. Most managers underutilized the internal messaging system since many did not want consumers to see them using their phones while on the floor. There were no shipping cost difficulties during this release. The strategic managers utilize this information to begin planning for the next new product launch.

CHAPTER 02

Start Building

Understand aspects of Strategy

Section 01

What to consider while building your Business Strategy

What to consider while building your Business Strategy

- **Defining your business strategy**

When beginning a firm, it is essential to consider your business plan carefully. This will be your map, which will assist you in choosing the path your firm will go and what the future holds. By having a well-defined strategy, you will have a framework and guiding principles that will assist you in growing your firm, achieving your objectives, and fostering its development.

Remember that you cannot supply everything to all of your consumers. Additionally, market dominance is not required to be a successful rival. Focusing on your business's capabilities and how you distinguish from rivals is the most crucial factor.

After establishing your company plan, you will have defined clear goals for your staff, which will help you attract and retain top personnel. Each team will have its duties and priorities. However, they should not conflict with the company's overall business plan.

You may document your company plan in a few paragraphs or as a series of statements. Your business plan is a statement of how your company will accomplish its goals, meet the demands of its customers, and retain a competitive market position within its industry. When presenting your company plan, it should address the following issues:

- Why does the organization exist?
- What are the organization's primary strengths?
- Which clientele should the organization prioritize?
- Which products/services are worthwhile to market, and which are not?
- Why were these strategic goals selected?

By answering these questions, you should be able to determine your organization's priorities.

• Organization's priorities

1. Clearly define your long-term objectives.

You should ensure that your organization's strategic plan is attainable and appropriate over the long run. Consider the kind of products or services you want to provide, who will be interested in buying them, which market you should target, and the activities you need to engage in to reach your goals and objectives.

2. The opportunity

Be mindful to analyze the many prospects available to you and how they may develop. Before making a final choice, amass facts, information, and statistics about these prospects. By considering all the potential dangers and obstacles associated with each opportunity, you will be better equipped to avoid or overcome them.

3. Innovation

When considering the items or services you want to provide, be careful to determine how they vary from the competitors and how they complement your business.

4. Competition

You must ensure that your company plan continues to be competitive. Choose an underserved or untapped market where you will face little to no competition when determining which market to enter. This is how you will canopy market space, build your brand, and make it more difficult for rivals to join your area.

5. *Economies of scale*

Are careful to reduce the price of your products or services as feasible while maintaining their effectiveness and originality. It is always preferable to provide excellent customer service and distinctive characteristics.

6. *Time to market*

Consider the choices for building instead of purchasing the products or services you are considering offering your customers. Sometimes it is less costly to purchase a portion of a product or service on the market or to source the job. This may occasionally reduce the cost of manufacturing and marketing the product or service in its entirety.

7. *Tests*

Ensure that you test your approach once it has been developed. Your strategy should always be feasible and consistent with your company's objectives and market demands. Take care to test it in stages. It is preferable to fail while the stakes are low than to make a major error later, when it would be far more difficult to recover.

8. *Risks and failures*

Consider the risks associated with your firm while formulating your plan and let yourself and your workers make errors and fail. This will provide you with useful knowledge and insight from which you can grow and achieve success.

9. *Stakeholders*

After completing the development of your plan, you should communicate it to your team. This will provide them with direction and a better knowledge of the steps the organization will take by its plan. Describe the relevance of your approach to their job inside the organization. Additionally, you should notify external stakeholders about your plan. Investors, suppliers, industry analysts, and partners must know your revenue generation and shareholder value influencing strategies.

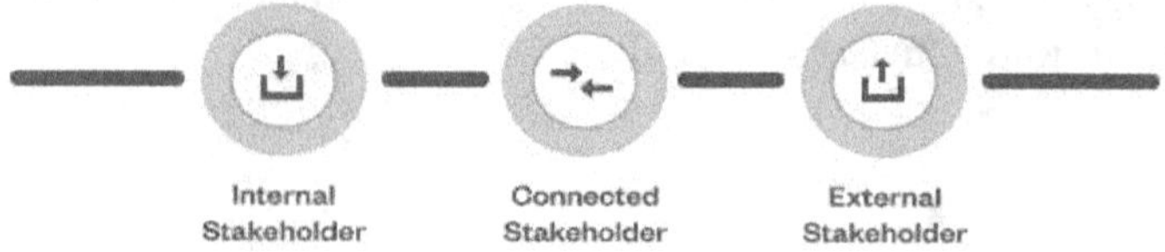

CHAPTER 02

Start Building

Understand aspects of Strategy

Section 02

Strategy Levels

Strategy Levels

- **Types of Strategy Levels**

There are three sorts of Strategy levels that may be implemented in a firm. Each contributes to a rise in profits and business cohesion.

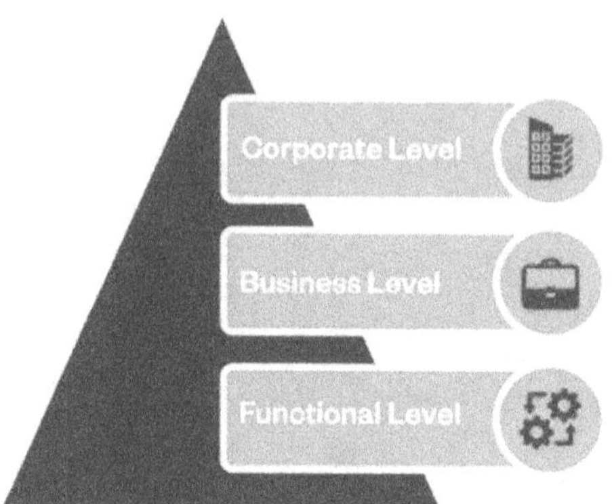

1. **Corporate level strategy:**
   This approach is adopted at the company's top level. Executives of a firm consider strategies to enhance and extend the business. They may find potential new markets to enter.

2. **Business level strategy:**

   This method focuses on implementing corporate ambitions inside individual business contexts.

3. **Functional level strategy:**

   This approach emphasizes the individual responsibilities of departments and people in achieving organizational objectives.

Corporate level strategy

CORPORATE LEVEL STRATEGY

STABILITY STRATEGY   EXPANSION STRATEGY   RETRENCHMENT STRATEGY   COMBINATION STRATEGY

- **What Is a Corporate-Level Strategy?**

A corporate-level strategy is a multi-tiered business plan that executives use to identify, describe, and attain specified business objectives. A small firm may utilize a corporate-level strategy to raise its earnings during the following fiscal year, but a big corporation may supervise the operations of numerous companies to accomplish more difficult objectives, such as selling the company or entering a new market.

- **Types of corporate-level strategy**

When building the corporate-level strategy for your business, you seek the most efficient means of allocating resources to meet the company's requirements and achieve its goals. It may also assist you in developing a contingency plan so that you are prepared to function under unpredictable conditions.
Let's examine the many corporate-level techniques that might be employed:

a. Stability strategy

The stability approach entails continuing to deal with customers inside your sector. This plan also implies that your company's present business model is successful. Due to the unpredictability of the route to growth, you should utilize a stability plan to assure incremental revenue-generating advances, such as research and development and product innovation. Offering free trials of your everyday items to your target audience is one way to enhance their engagement.

b. Expansion strategy

If your firm intends to create new items and reach new customers, the growth strategy is ideal for you. It may also be used to increase the activity inside a firm, for example, by acquiring more customers and recruiting additional workers. You may choose this method if the area in which you operate has a robust economy or if your primary objective is to improve performance. This technique provides a high earning potential for CEOs, which may lead to paying hikes and an extension of employee perks.

c. Retrenchment strategy

A retrenchment plan necessitates that you seriously contemplate a business model change. This may entail ceasing production or lowering a product's functioning. You may need to devote extra resources to accounts receivable to guarantee that you continue to get paid for the services you've rendered and sustain your firm's cash flow.
This method is only used when a firm wishes to preserve its solvency by taking precautionary steps. You should do a SWOT (Strengths, Weaknesses, Opportunities, and Threats) study to determine which marketing you can operate effectively.

d. Combined Strategy

A combination strategy is a blend of the three preceding business model strategies. Its primary objective is to improve the company's performance and determine which sectors may expand or contract depending on market circumstances. This technique makes it simpler to modify your strategy since you have more flexibility with your time and how much should be devoted to each strategy function.

• **Characteristics of a corporate-level strategy**

When contemplating the corporate-level strategy you should implement, keep the following examples in mind:

a. Diversification

Diversification is when you realize you need to shift your operational market. Entering new markets enables the creation of new business prospects with customers. It may allow you to establish a long-lasting connection based on the delivery and pleasure of your goods and services. If you have the funds, you might consider rebranding your services to a new audience willing to test a new offering.

b. Forward or backward integration

Forward integration is when a firm assumes the place of a prior participant in the supply chain. Your company's transformation into a distributor will alter the scope of your operations, and you will need to reallocate resources to assist in transporting and storing goods for local businesses. Backward integration entails beginning in the supply chain company and transitioning into a provider of products and services. To accommodate the shift in your company, you may need to create extra goods.

c. Horizontal integration

Occurs when two businesses in the same vertical unite. If you combine with another firm, you must ensure that you have the operational capability to manage the merger and work with new personnel eager to understand your processes and how they vary from those of the acquired company.

d. Profit

This approach is only focused on increasing spending capital once expenditures are deducted. You may need to minimize costs and expenditures by selling assets such as stocks and bonds, increasing the price of the services you provide to customers, and reducing non-essential services.

e. Turnaround

Refers to boosting the efficacy of current items to increase sales. To earn more revenue, you may need to improve your testing procedures and quality assurance standards to earn more revenue.

f. Divestment

Is a retrenchment approach aiming to fix issues and improve corporate performance. To generate funds and disclose good financial information to internal and external stakeholders, you begin by selling high-performing shares and paying off obligations.

g. Liquidation

Is the ultimate option available to business owners. This action will be taken when you have exhausted all other alternatives for increasing your business's earnings. This leads to the sale of your business to another entity and the discontinuation of all product lines.

h. Concentration

Is a growth strategy that increases market share in the industry in which you operate. It is considered a high-reward approach due to the market demand for the business you are entering.

i. Investigation

The inquiry involves evaluating expansion and contraction options. After prioritizing your performance or readjusting the scope of your firm, you'll be able to choose which approach to implement.

j. No change

The absence of change is often associated with your stability approach. To guarantee customer use and brand loyalty, it's essential to identify areas where your product must be improved.

Business level strategy

- ### What is a business-level strategy?

A business-level strategy is an innovative approach for a firm to highlight its distinctive advantages, enhance its competitive edge, and assist the organization's separate components in functioning as a unified whole. This strategy focuses on enhancing how departments communicate with one another and see their roles within the organization while establishing standards for achieving the overall objective.

- ### Examples of business-level strategies

There are four business-level strategies adaptable to your organization's objectives. The list below defines and analyzes these four examples of enterprise-level strategies:

a. Cost leadership strategy

The cost leadership approach is designed to discover the optimal price for a product based on customer preferences. Cost leadership strategy compels a company to consider the production, shipping, and customer delivery expenses that determine the price point at which they can sell their product and generate a profit. This approach aims to identify the most cost-efficient method to promote and sell a product to clients, hence beating rivals with higher price points.

b. Low-cost strategy

The low-cost approach prioritizes marketing to a specific market or company above the entire. e public. This technique is used like cost leadership, but it involves undercutting rivals so that companies see them as a more appealing and cost-effective alternative to purchase from.

c. Differentiation strategy

The differentiation approach improves a company's competitive position by emphasizing product quality rather than price. Companies that want customers to purchase their goods based on quality rather than price should set standards to increase the functioning and worth of their products.

d. Integrated strategy

The integrated approach combines the key elements of the low-cost and differentiation strategies to produce a product of average quality. Using this method, a corporation would attract clients who want the next-best level of quality at a lesser price than high-quality things.

• How to implement a business-level strategy

To create a successful business-level plan that will benefit your organization, you must identify and implement objectives in every department. To do this, you must have a comprehensive strategy in place. Below is a list of seven measures you may take to build a lucrative business-level plan for your organization.

a. Identify the target market and consumers.

Before implementing corporate improvements, you must first determine the target market you want to penetrate and your ideal clients.

Example: You are a provider of office supplies. You sell paper, writing implements, printers, and ink cartridges presently. You want to enter the office furniture industry and offer chairs, desks, and cubicles to develop your firm. Consider your rivals who have already joined this market. What are their costs? Who purchases their workplace furniture?

b. Find out what their needs are

Once you have determined your target market, the price of your competitors, and the ideal client base for that market, you can begin investigating your customer base's demands.

Example: Your office supply firm initiates consumer requirements research based on competition sales. The following questions will direct your study. What kinds of office furniture do they require? What kind of materials are they seeking? What is the pricing range for these products?

c. Discuss how to cater to their needs

Now that you know which materials and furniture items are in great demand among your target clients, you should collaborate with other business leaders to locate suppliers, debate delivery alternatives, and choose a pricing point that will set you apart from rivals.

Example: Your office supply firm investigates market trends to determine the most popular office furniture goods. Then, you call wholesalers and manufacturers to locate supplies and items within the budget you and your teammates established.

d. Make comparisons to competitor strategies

Analyze how your rivals keep expenses while generating a profit and retaining client loyalty. Examine the areas in which you may improve based on your comparisons.

Example: Your office supply firm continues its present strategy while analyzing rival models to see how they are changing and improving in response to market shifts in office furniture.

e. Set common goals to be met by the company

After performing the essential research to join a new market, you may begin to formulate company-wide objectives to increase your market potential.

Example: You and your colleagues at the corporate level recommend increasing the company's income by 25% by the end of the following fiscal year via increased office furniture sales.

f. Set unique department goals

Setting departmental objectives helps segregate the duties that might contribute to the overall success of your business. This stage requires effective communication between the corporate and workers to communicate department-specific activities.

Example: At the departmental level of your office supply firm, each department has been allocated certain objectives and targets to achieve.

The sales staff is responsible for promoting your company's office furniture items. The marketing team is responsible for developing awareness campaigns for this new version of your products.

g. Complete routine checks at each company level

After assigning distinct tasks to each department, you should conduct monthly reviews to ensure that progress is being made and that your original message has not been lost.

Functional Level Strategy

- **Definition, Types & Examples**

How do you accomplish your organization's annual objectives? Do you just establish an annual goal and then pursue it aimlessly? Or, do you establish milestones semiannually, monthly, weekly, or even daily? Which is the best strategy for achieving your long-term objectives? Defining short-term objectives is a more effective strategy for achieving long-term ones.

In addition, you need a plan to handle these normal or daily functional duties. In commercial words, you need a plan at the functional level. Want to learn more about its kinds, significance, and real-world applications? Well, if you do, keep reading!

- **What Is a Functional Level Strategy?**

A functional level strategy is an action plan to accomplish short-term, regular, or daily business objectives to support the corporate and business level plans. Essentially, a functional level plan helps a corporation handle every day or normal operational processes.

A functional level strategy encompasses many operational or functional domains, such as marketing, human resources, production, research and development, sales, etc.

In addition, functional units often design their functional strategies. The following components are essential for a functional level strategy:

It should represent the organizational and operational objectives/goals. It must provide optimal resource allocation across all functional areas/units.

A functional level plan must maximize cooperation across all functional domains to achieve their outputs.

- **Why is Functional Level Strategy Important?**

Any company must have a functional level plan for the following reasons:

- It serves as stepping stones for achieving corporate and business-level goals.

A functional level strategy aids in the development of a layout for performing routine/everyday company processes.
- It works as a binding factor in every corporation; it combines multiple functional/operational divisions such as human resources, marketing, sales, research and development, manufacturing, customer relations, etc.
- Micro-level functional methods are more pragmatic/practical and assist in coping with any real issue (in an organization).

• Features of Functional Strategies

Here are a few essential characteristics of a functional level strategy:

- Unlike commercial or corporate plans, functional level strategies have a shorter duration.
- It outlines the steps a corporation must take to implement the grand plan.
  Every functional level strategy has the ultimate purpose of pursuing the company strategy.
- It applies to an organization's department, function, and division.
- Functional level strategies also address sub-functional domains (if any).
- Each functional unit or department formulates its functional plan by directives at a higher level.
- In the hierarchy, functional level strategies are at the bottom.
- They support the company strategy, which in turn supports the enterprise strategy.
- The primary emphasis of functional-level tactics is the external environment.
- A functional level strategy may vary throughout locations of the same company. i.e. many business units/franchises in various regions/cities/states.
- Each functional unit's strategy must be tightly integrated to achieve the corporation's overarching goals.

• Factors of Functional Level Strategy

a. Alignment

As previously stated, a functional-level plan must match the business and corporate-level strategies. If the company's purpose is to enhance profits.

b. Integration

Horizontal implementation of functional-level techniques is required. This facilitates the integration of various functional units, resulting in greater efficiency.

c. Existing Resources

Each department, division, or functional unit must have sufficient resources, such as money, personnel, etc., to execute a functional level strategy.

d. Progress

Due to an abundance of data, measuring the performance of a functional approach may be complicated. Therefore, it is crucial that how and what kind of data be monitored to determine whether or not progress has been made.

• Examples of functional level strategy type

There are many significant forms of functional level tactics, such as:

a. Marketing Strategies

Marketing has become one of the most crucial functional areas of every firm. Although marketing is a huge topic in and of itself, it focuses mostly on understanding the requirements of a target market and then providing goods or services to meet those needs. A marketing strategy comprises several components, but the marketing mix (product, price, location, and promotion) is likely the most crucial.

There are a variety of marketing tactics available today, such as relationship marketing, social marketing, location marketing, person marketing, and direct marketing, among others.

Now, if the corporate-level strategy focuses on Quality, Delivery, and Efficiency, the responses of various organizational divisions are as follows:

Example

Quality	Offering useful deliverables.
Delivery	Responding promptly to the fluctuating seasonal demands of customers.
Efficiency	The next marketing effort should target the appropriate demographic.

b. *Financial Strategies*

Financial strategy encompasses every aspect of financial management. The strategy focuses primarily on the planning, acquiring, using, and managing of a company's financial resources. A financial strategy addresses issuing/raising cash, purchasing assets, investments, budgeting, managing working capital, applying funds, dividend payment, etc.

Example

Quality	Inputting data and distributing it to other functional units with no or minimal mistakes.
Delivery	Ensuring real-time data access.
Efficiency	Accounting/finance procedures are automated.

c. *Production Strategies*

A production plan oversees all aspects of the manufacturing process. This method encompasses manufacturing systems, supply chain management, logistics, and operational planning and control. The fundamental purpose of a manufacturing plan are:

- Enhance the quality,
- Minimizing the overall manufacturing cost,
- Increasing amount.

Example

Quality	Enhancement of production process's quality.
Delivery	reducing time wastage.
Efficiency	Reducing/controlling manufacturing process delays.

d. Human Resource Strategies

Human resource strategy at a company encompasses all aspects of the business's workforce. The fundamental job of any HR department is to foster the growth of workers and provide them with adequate working circumstances and chances for advancement so that they may contribute to achieving corporate objectives. HR includes recruiting, training, motivation, development, and employee retention.

Example

Quality	Regular training programs for skill improvement
Delivery	Assuring a timely recruiting and hiring procedure to satisfy the workforce requirements of the firm.
Efficiency	Cost-effective recruiting and hiring procedures

e. Research & Development Strategies

A R&D strategy focuses primarily on two factors:

- *Innovation; product development*
- *Making enhancements to existing items*

To execute various business strategies, such as market penetration, concentric diversification, and product development, a company must continually introduce new items and enhance existing ones. There are typically three R&D methodologies for implementing these ideas;

- Be the pioneer; offer a revolutionary product;
- Produce inexpensive goods;
- Be a savvy, inventive follower;
- add additional features and offer a product that is comparable to the competition but superior.

Quality	Creating novel goods that enhance the client experience.
Delivery	Implement parallel design strategies to decrease time to market.
Efficiency	Simplify R&D procedures.

Example

• Examples of Functional Strategies

Yahoo- Marissa Mayer's Failure to Understand Company's Functional levels

a. History

Yahoo (a former industry powerhouse) recruited Marissa Mayer, a renowned and successful Google executive, hoping that she would reverse Yahoo's "struggling" fortunes. Initially, the investors were confident she could rescue the firm from "black depths." However, what occurred was entirely unexpected for everyone.
Marissa's largest error was complete ignorance of the corporation's functional and operational levels. She did propose other modifications, but she misjudged the pushback from Yahoo's lower-level staff to these changes.

b. The Outcome

After all, her efforts were futile. She advocated Yahoo's sale as the best option. Verizon paid barely $5 billion to purchase Yahoo, a previously $135 billion firm.

CHAPTER 02

Start Building

Understand aspects of Strategy

Section 03

Ten measures you may follow to develop & implement the most effective company strategies

Ten measures you may follow to develop and implement the most effective company strategies

1. Develop a true vision

Vision is an abstract term with varying definitions for various individuals. A vision or vision statement is traditionally a glimpse of the future. It should contain objectives for the organization you want to be and, unlike a mission statement, clearly defines what success entails (customers, markets, volume, etc.).

2. Define competitive advantage

The core of the strategy is determining how a business can provide distinctive value to its consumers. In many economic areas, businesses are mired in a sea of uniformity. A well-considered business plan should analyze how a firm may differentiate itself from the competitors via its service offering, price model, and delivery method, among other factors.

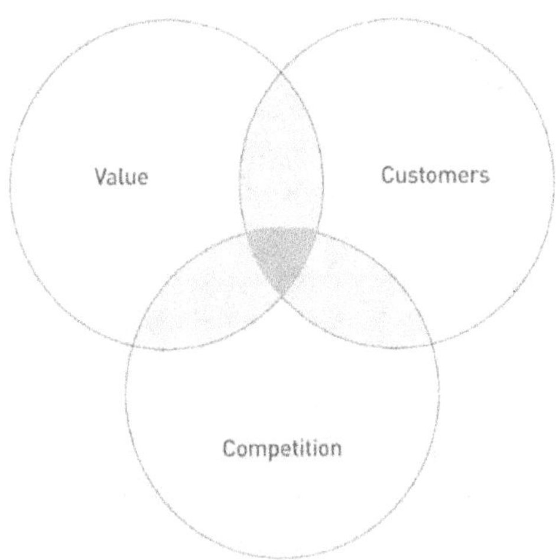

3. Define your targets

Poor targeting is one of the significant hurdles to progress. Without highly specified objectives, firms suffer from ambiguous messaging and misalignment between marketing and sales. Defining niches and specializations enables businesses to concentrate resources (of course, some companies are generalists by design).
A company's capacity to build an integrated sales and marketing strategy is contingent on distinct target markets; marketing supports sales productivity. When sales and marketing objectives are tight, strategies are performed more successfully.

4. Focus on systematic growth

According to one of our customer members, "a flourishing business is a growing business." Only via expansion can businesses afford to spend on items such as technology, the most exemplary employees, and new equipment. The strategic strategy should specify which areas a business will develop and in what percentage, such that the product mix provides a certain net margin.
Only after reaching such findings might a corporation determine how much it can spend on CAPEX, overhead expenditures, etc.

5. Make fact-based decisions

Strategy is a case of trash in, rubbish out. Executives often lament a dearth of usable data, yet we regularly uncover the knowledge that aids in formulating strategy.

Once, we collaborated with a Vistage member attempting to measure the worth of different customer categories. By obtaining the public records of a neighboring port, we could quantify prospective clients' real shipments of items.

6.   Think long-term

Due to ongoing change, planning horizons are now shorter than they formerly were. However, focusing just quarterly might hinder a company's capacity to anticipate future events. Best-in-class businesses develop procedures that regard strategy as a yearly cycle rather than a single, static event.

7.   But be nimble

Companies may be both long-sighted and agile. An understanding of external factors, for example, is a crucial element of strategy. Companies should evaluate long-term external pressures and pivot depending on new knowledge (frequent meetings, possibly quarterly).

Amazon's Jeff Bezos hosts a strategy meeting every Tuesday to keep it at the forefront of his management's minds.

8.   Be inclusive

To remain adaptable, businesses employ a broader range of personnel than in the past. There is more openness at a time when corporations are employing more millennials. While I would never call for corporations to reveal their finances (since that is a business owner's choice), there is a trend toward more inclusiveness and openness.

Whom to involve in the creation of a plan is a crucial decision. We advise company owners to employ individuals they can rely on and think strategically.

9.   Invest time in pre-work

If you want your managers to take strategy seriously, require them to undertake research and compile pertinent data before your strategy sessions.

10. Measure your results and execute excellently

Every approach must be executable. Companies that are industry leaders:

Have a strategic action plan that is often monitored (usually monthly).
Promote shared plan ownership among leaders and divisions.
Utilize predictive key performance indicators (KPIs) that closely connect
with the strategic goal.
Have objectives cascade to each department and resonate with workers,
so they understand how their position contributes to the organization's
overall mission.
Establish a company schedule that encourages productive meetings and a
performance management cycle that facilitates each employee's
cascading of goals and objectives.
Every year, they rinse and redo their strategic cycle.

Senior executives are responsible for promoting practices that keep a
team focused on the goal since strategic planning execution demands
discipline.

CHAPTER 02

Start Building

Understand aspects of Strategy

Section 04

Strategy Implementation

Strategy Implementation

In the ever-evolving landscape of business, the ability to formulate a robust strategy is only half the battle. True success lies in the effective implementation of those strategies. Welcome to the world of strategy implementation – a critical aspect of organizational management that ensures that the well-crafted plans translate into tangible results. In this exploration, we will delve into the key components, challenges, and best practices of strategy implementation, equipping beginners with the essential knowledge to navigate this intricate terrain.

• Understanding Strategy Implementation

At its core, strategy implementation is the process of executing and operationalizing strategic plans. It involves translating the overarching goals and objectives of an organization into specific actions, allocating resources, and aligning the workforce towards the common goal. While strategy formulation focuses on decision-making and planning, implementation is the hands-on, day-to-day execution that transforms vision into reality.

• Key Components of Strategy Implementation

a. Clear Communication

Effective strategy implementation begins with clear communication. Leaders must articulate the strategic objectives, the rationale behind them, and the role each individual play in achieving them. Transparency builds trust and ensures that everyone is working towards a common purpose.

b. Strategic Leadership

Strong leadership is paramount during implementation. Leaders must inspire and motivate teams, foster a culture of accountability, and be agile in responding to challenges. The alignment of leadership styles with the strategic objectives ensures a smoother implementation process.

c. *Resource Alignment*

Allocating resources – human, financial, and technological – in line with the strategic priorities is a crucial step. Organizations need to ensure that they have the right people with the right skills, adequate funding, and the necessary technology to support the execution of the strategy.

d. *Performance Metrics and Monitoring*

Establishing key performance indicators (KPIs) is essential for tracking progress. Regular monitoring and evaluation enable organizations to identify deviations from the plan early on, allowing for timely adjustments and improvements.

e. *Adaptability and Flexibility*

The business environment is dynamic, and unforeseen challenges are inevitable. A successful strategy implementation requires organizations to be adaptable and flexible. A willingness to revise strategies based on changing circumstances is a hallmark of effective implementation.

- ## **Challenges in Strategy Implementation**

a. *Resistance to Change*

Employees may resist changes that come with strategy implementation, leading to decreased morale and productivity. Addressing concerns, communicating the benefits of the changes, and involving employees in the process can help mitigate resistance.

b. *Poor Communication*

Inadequate communication can result in misunderstandings and misalignment. Ensuring that information flows effectively across all levels of the organization is crucial for successful implementation.

c. *Lack of Resources*

Insufficient resources, whether financial, human, or technological, can impede the execution of a strategy. Proper resource allocation and realistic planning are essential to avoid this challenge.

d. Ineffective Leadership

Leadership that is indecisive, unresponsive, or inconsistent can hinder the implementation process. Strong and adaptive leadership is necessary to guide the organization through the complexities of strategy execution.

• Best Practices for Successful Strategy Implementation

a. Engage Stakeholders

Involving key stakeholders, both internal and external, in the strategy implementation process fosters a sense of ownership and commitment. Their insights and support can significantly contribute to successful execution.

b. Continuous Learning and Improvement

Strategy implementation is an iterative process. Regularly assess performance, learn from both successes and failures, and make necessary adjustments. A culture of continuous improvement ensures sustained success.

c. Employee Training and Development

Equip your workforce with the skills and knowledge required to meet the demands of the new strategy. Investing in training and development programs ensures that employees are prepared for their evolving roles.

d. Celebrate Successes

Recognize and celebrate achievements, no matter how small. Acknowledging successes boosts morale, reinforces a positive culture, and encourages continued commitment to the strategic goals.

• Conclusion

In the complex realm of strategic management, mastering strategy implementation is the key to turning vision into reality. By understanding the components, recognizing challenges, and adopting best practices, beginners can embark on a journey towards successful strategy execution. Remember, effective implementation is a dynamic and continuous process, requiring commitment, adaptability, and a relentless pursuit of excellence. As you navigate the intricacies of strategy implementation, may this guide be your companion on the path to organizational success.